RIGHT: CMB XF 26 former DMS 374 is seen in Des Voeux Road Central outside the construction site of the new Headquarters of the Hong Kong and Shanghai Bank the front number plate is now in the later style of black numbers on a white reflective background.

29 October 1984

1984年10月29日，中巴 XF26 (前倫敦寶 374)，已換上全新白色反光車牌，駛經香港上海滙豐銀行現址的地盤。

CENTRE: CMB XF 76 former DMS 836 seen in an identical spot to the previous photograph; note the differing upper deck window treatment compared with XF 26.

29 October 1984

在同學位置拍攝的中巴XF76，其上層車廂格式，與XF26的格局截然不同，此圖攝於 1984年10月29日。

BELOW: Central bus station before it was covered over by the new buildings forming Exchange Square. Both vehicles have received modified windows on the lower deck front which incorporate openings so necessary for work in a hot climate. XF 109 former DMS 857 stands next to XF 92 former DMS 875.

29 October 1984

爲提供較涼快的駕駛環境，XF109 及 XF92 的下層前幅玻璃被更換，以全新的模樣於尚未興建成交易廣場的中環總站示人。

DMSColourScene
HONG KONG
Foreword

This is the first book in a planned series covering my personal photographs of the DMS class of Daimler Fleetlines new to London Transport which were exported to Hong Kong for further use. Towards the end of this book I include some photographs taken in Guangzhou of vehicles formerly used in Hong Kong that were sent to mainland China for additional use. More photographs taken in mainland China will appear in the next book.

My first visit to Hong Kong was made in November 1984 and further visits were made in most years until 1998 by which time only a few DMSs remained in service in either Hong Kong or China. Following my first visit it was clear that I would need more detailed information on operators and their garages before a second visit. Accordingly I made contact with Ron Phillips of the PSV Circle who put me in touch with Mike Davis who had recently returned to the UK after many years in Hong Kong. He was able to provide considerable help in preparation for my second visit in 1985 and provided contact names and locations for the four main operators of DMSs in Hong Kong, namely Citybus, Argos, CMB and KMB. Armed with this information, and continued assistance from both Mike and Ron, I was subsequently able to include visits to the various depots as well as the usual on-street locations. In particular I wish to thank Lyndon Rees, MBE, and subsequently Tim Phillips and Stuart Dobie, all of Citybus for their help not just with vehicles in their own fleet, but also for giving me details on the other operators. In respect of the other fleets the following all provided help and allowed various depot visits: CMB, Jim Sykes. KMB Training School, Eric Montgomery. Argos, John Lane and Clement Lau.

In respect of the visits to Guangzhou I am extremely grateful to Lennox MacEwan, OBE, who provided details including maps of the city and encouraged my visits, without such assistance I doubt whether I would have made such visits.

Anyone who has visited Hong Kong will know that it is quite difficult to photograph buses in service other than at terminal points due to heavy traffic, street furniture and the use of fareboxes such that buses only stop very briefly at bus stops, nearside views of buses on the move are thus rare. Nevertheless I hope you find this selection of photographs represents the scene in Hong Kong during the period and shows that the DMS was an important part of the bus scene there.

Finally, in addition to the help provided by Mike Davis prior to each visit I acknowledge the considerable help and advice from him in his current position as owner of DTS Publishing that allowed this book to be produced.

February 2002

Nigel Eadon-Clarke
Chislehurst
Kent
UK

All photographs by the Author – Translated by He Jiawei

BELOW: Operating on a contract for the JDH office building in the former Hung Hum dockyard is Citybus 43 former DMS 2165 standing at Hung Hom ferry pier. A photograph of this vehicle in Guangzhou appears later in this book. **13 November 1990**

城巴的D43這天行駛JDH公司的黃埔船廠之員工接駁巴士路線，停泊於紅磡碼頭外，此車在1990年代出售至廣州一汽，它在廣州服務的照片可在本書稍後部分找到。

First published 2002
ISBN: 1 900515 60 1
Publishe.. by DTS, PO Box 105, Croydon, UK
Printed by Fretwells Print & Design, Keighley, West Yorkshire

DTS Publishing

British Library Cataloguing in Publication Data. A catalogue record for this book is available from the British Library.

London Jumbos – 倫敦寶 / Lun Tun Bo

When the first batch of CMB Fleetlines (LF-class) entered service in 1974, they were dubbed Jumbos by their operator. The name was obviously a reference to their high passenger carrying capacity which was quite impressive at that time for two-axle buses. Since then, Hong Kong bus enthusiasts have associated the term Jumbo with the Fleetline chassis. In their jargon, Metsec-bodied Fleetlines are known as 圓頂寶 (Yuen Ding Bo, literally, round roofed Jumbos because of the rounded roof domes) whereas the more angular looking BACO-bodied Fleetlines are called 平頂寶 (Ping Ting Bo, literally, flat top Jumbos). Last but not least, the heroes of this book, the ex-LT Fleetlines, though long withdrawn from service, are still fondly remembered here as "London Jumbos" (倫敦寶 / Lun Tun Bo).

FRONT COVER: A typical Hong Kong scene, CMB XF 53 is former DMS 617 it stands outside Statue Square in Chater Road Central surrounded by office buildings. Behind is CMB LX 201 notable as being the first Guy Arab V rebuilt with an Alexander body in 1977. This bus was returned by CMB to Alexander as a chassis for the fitting of the new body. The chassis had been new to Wolverhampton Corporation in 1963 as 7112UK. **27 November 1986**
典型的香港情景: 中巴XF53(前倫敦寶617)這天停在寫字樓(辦公室)大廈林立的遮打道附近的皇后像廣場外。其後的是中巴LX201，它是第一部配上亞力山大車身的重建佳牌阿拉伯五型巴士。它原是胡弗咸頓的7112UK，在1963年投入服務。中巴把它的底盤運回;英國在1977年完成裝配新的車身。

FRONTISPIECE: A typical scene in Central in the mid eighties. CMB XF 145 former DM 998 stops next to a tram in Des Voeux Road. The bus has been in Hong Kong for almost two years and the original style white on red number plate is carried on the front. **28 October 1984**
80年代中區常見的情景，在港服務近兩年的中巴XF145，被套上80年代初典型的紅底白字的車牌，駛經德輔道中. (此圖攝於1984年10月28日)。

BELOW: Citybus 45 was former DMS 2207 seen here at Ocean Park. This bus had originally been purchased by TSW Ltd for operation in Macau before entering service with Citybus earlier in 1986. This bus would later see further service in Guangzhou, compare with other photographs in this book taken on 15 November 1985 and 5 May 1992. **25 November 1986**
城巴45同樣停泊於海洋公園外;此車原來由澳門福利汽車公司所購入，於1986年初轉售至城巴，其後亦被易手至廣州一汽繼續服務廣州市民

色彩繽紛倫敦寶

DMS ColourScene

HONG KONG

N. J. Eadon-Clarke

Translated into Chinese by

DTS Publishing

LEFT: CMB XF 176 former DM 1215 had been in service in Hong Kong for one year when it was captured on film in the Central bus station. Apart from the full depth sliding windows fitted on each side the bus appears little modified from its 'London' condition. The red exact money farebox can be seen through the windscreen.

29 October 1984

XF176 (前倫敦寶 1215) 在港服役近一年，全車的車窗已被更換成全幅的推拉式，從下層車窗內觀望，紅色的錢箱顯而易見(此圖攝於1984年10月29日)。

CENTRE: CMB XF 70, former DMS 743; the bar across the rear part of the front door locking that part permanently shut can be seen.

29 October 1984

前閘的後端被鐵棒封閉爲中巴倫敦寶的一大特色，XF70 (前倫敦寶 743) 爲典型的例子，此圖攝於1984年10月29日。

LEFT: Different destination aperture treatment is evident on these two vehicles seen in the Central bus station, CMB XF 150 former DM 993 stands next to XF 192 former DMS 2086. XF 192 had entered Hong Kong service only a few days before this photograph was taken and the additional window fitted behind the front entrance door can clearly be seen.

29 October 1984

在1984年10月29日，剛被中巴編爲 XF192 的前倫敦寶 2086，前閘的後端被改建爲車窗的格局，這天與 XF150 同時攝於中環總站。

LEFT: Providing a contrast in both destination aperture and windscreen treatment are CMB XF 152 former DM 1058 and XF 87 former DMS 802 standing between duties at Central bus station.

29 October 1984

停泊在中環總站的XF152(前倫敦寶1058)，其路線牌箱及前幅玻璃的形狀，與毗鄰的XF87成了很大的對比。

BELOW: A typically busy traffic scene in Connaught Road Central sees CMB XF 173 former DM 1193 and red and silver Hong Kong taxi cabs.

29 October 1984

XF173在84年10月29日與一輛市區的士駛經繁忙的德輔道中。

LEFT: CMB XF 122 former DMS 897 seen in Connaught Road Central in an all over advertisement livery for Salem cigarettes. Behind the bus can be seen hoardings advertising the forthcoming development of Exchange Square which would eventually cover over the Central bus station making photographs at that location almost impossible.

29 October 1984

全車已披上沙龍香煙廣告的XF122同樣駛經德輔道中；車後的交易廣告場巨幅廣告提示我們竣工後的廣場將完全覆蓋中環總站。

ABOVE: Citybus D 28 former DMS 2155 seen in the attractive MTR livery in Connaught Road Central. This bus would later see further service in Guangzhou, see photograph dated 5 May 1992 later in this book.

29 October 1984

城巴 D28 (前倫敦寶2155) 於 1984 年髹鐵色彩駛經德輔道中，此車於90被運往廣州服役。

RIGHT: Attractive liveried Argos 21 former DMS 184 stands outside the Star Ferry terminal on Hong Kong island while working a free shuttle service to a new shopping development named Cityplaza at Tai Koo. The forthcoming opening of the MTR Island Line would negate the need for such a service.

29 October 1984

雅高巴士於80年代初提供由太至中環天星碼頭的免費穿梭巴務．於 1984年10月29日，披上漂亮的前倫敦寶 184 (雅高21號)，行走此

RIGHT: Numerically the first DMS acquired by KMB was 2D8 former DMS 725 it is seen here arriving at the Star Ferry Kowloon in an all over advertisement livery. This bus would later pass to Speedybus and see further service in Guangzhou see photograph dated 5 May 1992 later in this book.

前倫敦寶725爲九巴第一部引進敦寶，編號爲2D8，2D8於80年級必達巴士購入，服務廣州市民。

LEFT: A new lower front panel alters the frontal appearance of KMB 2D27 former DMS 727 as it arrives at the Star Ferry Kowloon, the large side fleetname was unusual.

29 October 1984

九巴替旗下的倫敦寶2D27進行整容，下層裝上了簇新的前幅，這天駛至尖沙咀碼頭。

CENTRE LEFT: Central bus station Hong Kong sees CMB XF 187, former DM 1164, on busy route 6 to Stanley on the south side of the Island.

29 October 1984

自80年代中，不少中巴的倫敦寶被編往行走繁忙的6號路線，來往南區的赤柱至中環，XF187爲其中一員。

LEFT: CMB XF 71 former DMS 167 had been the last DMS delivered to LT with headlights close together as seen in this view in the Central bus station. The rear part of the front doors can be seen locked shut by a horizontal bar.

29 October 1984

中巴的XF71(前倫敦寶167)，爲最後一輛交付LT的倫敦寶，其車頭燈的距離較一般爲狹窄，而XF71前閘的後部份亦被鐵棒所封閉。

RIGHT: CMB XF 111 former DMS 913 stand in the Central bus station underneath a pedestrian walkway, note the less common destination aperture arrangement.
30 October 1984
XF111的路線顯示牌的格局較爲早見，這天它停泊於中環總站的行人路上。

BELOW: Sandwiched between the tram tracks and a road flyover in Queensway we see CMB XF 30 former DMS 481.
31 October 1984
XF30正行經金鐘道途中，在天橋與電車路間駛過。

RIGHT: CMB XF 145 former DM 998 pauses in Queensway on its way back to Central.
31 October 1984
前倫敦寶998被中巴購入後，旋即被編爲XF145，這天在金鐘道稍作停留。

RIGHT: A rear view of CMB XF 170 former DM 1202 in Queensway showing the removal of the engine in-fill panels and signs of oil leakage from the engine cover. To the right, tram no. 62 passes by en-route to Kennedy Town.

31 October 1984

從XF170的後幅，整個車尾的格式與引擎蓋上的油漬顯而易見．旁邊爲駛往堅尼地城總站的62號電車。

CENTRE RIGHT: Citybus D26 former DMS 2145 in the attractive MTR livery seen in Canton Road Kowloon. This bus would be sold to Argos for further service.

31 October 1984

全車髹上地鐵色彩的城巴D26，這天駛經九龍廣東道，此車其後由雅高巴士購入。

BELOW: With centre door removed, but otherwise looking very much like it did when in service with London Transport Argos No. 14 former DM 1746 speeds along Kowloon Park Drive Kowloon.

31 October 1984

被封閉了中門的雅高巴士14號，這天於九龍公園徑上飛馳。

LEFT: Freshly repainted CMB XF 35 former DMS 30 stands in the Central bus station clearly showing its close together headlights.

31 October 1984

於 1984 年底，剛翻新的中巴 XF35 停泊於中環總站，距離較窄的車頭燈仍未被更換。

CENTRE LEFT: CMB XF 5 former DMS 453 stands at the Macau ferry terminal next to a KMB Duple bodied coach used on services to Kai Tak airport.

1 November 1984

XF5 這天與九巴都普車身的機場豪華巴士一同停泊於港澳碼頭側。

BELOW: In the shadow of high rise buildings and running over the tram tracks we see CMB XF 173 former DM 1193 opposite the Macau ferry terminal.

1 November 1984

XF173 駛入於港澳碼頭對面的電車線內。

LEFT: The driver is in the process of changing the destination display in this view of CMB XF 187 former DM 1164 at the Stanley Prison terminus on the southern tip of Hong Kong island.

1 November 1984

停泊於赤柱監獄巴士總站外的 XF187，司機正轉動顯示目的地的布牌。

BELOW: KMB 2D50 former DMS 749 seen from an overhead pedestrian walkway in Kwun Tong Road Kowloon.

2 November 1984

2D50 在 1984年11月上旬駛經繁忙的觀塘道。

LEFT: KMB 2D49 former DMS 757 seen also in Kwun Tong Road showing the 'standard' condition of most KMB DMSs, the writing on the side of the vehicle asks that you do not overload the bus.

2 November 1984

不少九巴倫敦寶車身的兩旁，均髹上超載屬違例，乘客請合作"的標語，2D50 爲其中之一，這天同樣於觀塘道駛過。

ABOVE: Rear of MTR liveried Citybus D 28 former DMS 2155 (see also photograph taken on 29 October 1984) seen outside HMS Tamar and the Prince of Wales Building, the headquarters of the Ministry of Defence in Hong Kong.

4 November 1984

披上地鐵色彩的城巴D28，這天駛至金鐘，後方爲香港的前軍事重地—添馬艦及威爾斯大樓。

CENTRE RIGHT: The varied frontal treatment is obvious in this view taken in the Central bus station CMB XF 78 former DMS 721 stands next to un-numbered XF 152 former DM 1058.

5 November 1984

已被重建整幅擋風玻璃的XF78，這天與未寫上編組的XF152相遇於中環總站。

RIGHT: Citybus D29 former DMS 2154 was one of many Citybus vehicles in Ocean Park livery since Citybus held the contract to transport visitors from Central to the park on the south side of the Island. It is seen outside the park entrance.

5 November 1904

自城巴取得來往海洋公園至中環的接駁巴士的經營權後，不少城巴被髹上海洋公園的色彩，城巴的D29亦不例外，這天駛至海洋公園的正門。

LEFT: Having only just entered service Argos 31 former DMS 2124 in parked near Ocean Park in its original yellow paint scheme.

5 November 1984

於1984年初被編爲雅高巴士31號的前倫敦寶2124，以傳統雅高巴士黃色的色彩，駛至海洋公園。

BELOW LEFT: Citybus D41 former DMS 2130 stands at Kowloon railway station in MTR livery showing the retention of full width entrance and exit doors.

6 November 1984

城巴的D41上落車門均被保留原貌，這天抵達九龍火車總站。

ABOVE: Showing the revised rear light arrangement KMB 2D9 former DMS 739 the second KMB DMS numerically heads along Chatham road in south Kowloon.

6 November 1984

車尾燈經過修改後的九巴2D9，爲原來的倫敦寶739，這天行經尖沙咀漆咸道。

LEFT: Two very smart looking Argos DMSs stand behind the famous Peninsula hotel in Kowloon. Recently licenced No. 30 former DMS 2123 stands in front of No. 11 former DM 1784.

6 November 1984

兩部外貌突出的雅高巴士倫敦寶停泊於半島酒店旁，前者爲編號30(前身爲倫敦寶2123)，後者爲編號11(前身爲倫敦寶1784)。

RIGHT: The rear of Argos No. 11 former DM 1784 with DMS 2123 in the front behind the Peninsula hotel Kowloon while working on a contract private hire.

6 November 1984

停泊在後方的雅高巴士11號，這天提供私人租賃服務。

BELOW: Middle Road Kowloon was a terminal point for services to mainland China, it was also used for various other 'special' services. Argos gained a contract to transport visitors to Millies Discount Warehouse. They painted several vehicles in an appropriate advertising livery. Here we see No. 15 former DM 1878 behind No. 24 former DMS 301.

6 November 1984

尖沙咀中間道爲80年代不少提供特別服務及過境服務的巴士停泊地點。雅高巴士於1980年代爲妙麗批發中心提供穿梭巴士服務，並披上全幅的車身廣告。

ABOVE RIGHT: Argos No. 15 former DM 1878 stands in Middle Road Kowloon while working on the special free bus service to Millies Discount Warehouse.

6 November 1984

雅高15號巴士停泊於中間道，同樣爲妙麗批發中心提供免費巴士服務。

RIGHT: The rear of Argos No. 24 former DMS 301 in Middle Road Kowloon.

6 November 1984

雅高24號巴士同樣於1984年11月6日行駛妙麗批發中心提供之免費穿梭巴士服務。

TOP: Pursued by a KMB Dominant airport coach we see KMB 2D27 former DMS 727 in Nathan Road Kowloon, note the revised lower front panel and windscreen.

6 November 1984

在九巴機場豪華巴士後方的九巴2D27，這天一同駛經彌敦道；2D27的前幅與擋風玻璃經已被調低。

ABOVE: KMB 2D21 former DMS 765 retaining its original front and windscreen seen in Nathan Road Kowloon. This bus would go on to spend many years in the KMB driver training school see photograph dated 28 April 1992 later in this book.

6 November 1984

九巴2D21以原裝前幅的模樣駛經彌敦道。2D21後來被改裝成九巴車長訓練巴士，並服務一段長時間。

LEFT: Unlike CMB which only received PRV bodied examples half those received by KMB had MCW bodies, represented here by 2D83 former DMS 1592 seen in Nathan Road Kowloon.

6 November 1984

九巴2D21以原裝前幅的模樣駛經彌敦道。2D21後來被改裝成九巴車長訓練巴士，並服務一段長時間。

ABOVE: KMB 2D9 former DMS 739 arrives at the Star Ferry Kowloon on well known DMS route 2c.
6 November 1984
九巴第二部購入的倫敦寶2D9，於1984年11月6日行走路線2C，駛至尖沙咀碼頭總站。

RIGHT Rear view of KMB 2D9 former DMS 739 at the Star Ferry Kowloon terminus.
6 November 1984
攝於尖沙咀天星碼頭的九巴2D9後幅樣。

LEFT: A rare view of Citybus L14 former DMS 798 in yellow and cream livery standing at Admiralty bus station.
8 November 1984
城巴L14於1984年披上早見的奶黃色車身，駛至金鐘總站。

LEFT: Rear view of the first numerically DMS with KMB 2D8 former DMS 725 at the Star Ferry Kowloon terminus.

8 November 1984

九巴第一部引進的倫敦寶2D8，這天停於尖沙咀碼頭。

BELOW: KMB 2D82 former DMS 728 in bright sunshine in Nathan Road Kowloon.

8 November 1984

九巴的倫敦寶2D82(前倫敦寶728)，正行經陽光普照的彌敦道。

LEFT: CMB XF 10 former DMS 443 on route 24 squeezes down a narrow Hollywood Road in the Hong Kong mid-levels.

9 November 1984

行走中巴24號路線的XF10，沿著狹窄的荷里活道駛上香港半山區。

RIGHT: Another MCW bodied KMB DMS was 2D90 former DMS 1571 seen at the Star Ferry Kowloon with a large cruise liner in the background.
9 November 1984.
另一部配有MCW車身的2D90，在尖沙咀碼頭與背後的大型遠洋郵輪相映成趣。

RIGHT: CMB XF 22 former DMS 480 is taking a break at the bus stand by the Star Ferry, after over five years service with CMB it retains its original windscreen and apart from the full depth opening side windows and front bumper it remains very similar in appearance compared with its days with London Transport.
11 November 1985
中巴XF22於中環天星碼頭巴士站稍作停　留，直至1985年，其弧形的擋風玻璃仍被保留，除了推拉式車窗及前端的防撞橫外，XF22的模樣與其在英國服務時的外貌大同小異。

RIGHT: Citybus L12 former DMS 788 stands at the Star Ferry in the striking colour scheme before undertaking a trip to Ocean Park on the south side of the island. The 'L' indicates that it has retained its leyland engine.
11 November 1985
城巴L12停泊於中環天星碼頭，準備接載乘客到達海洋公園，後方的標記印證出此車仍使用利蘭原裝引擎。

ABOVE: KMB 2D93 former DMS 1565 is passed by Bristol built KMB Olympian BL2 in Nathan Road Kowloon. BL2 has an ECW body built in Lowestoft and had been licensed for service in July 1981 just one month before DMS 1565 which explains the similar number plates.

11 November 1985

九巴2D93 (前倫敦寶1565) 與九巴ECW車身的9.5米奧林比安BL2相遇於彌敦道；2D93與BL2同樣在1981年中服役。

CENTRE LEFT: Citybus began cross border route 500 in January 1985 with DMS vehicles. Here Citybus D36 former DMS 2157 stands at the Hong Kong start point for the route, Middle Road Kowloon. The additional Chinese number plate can be seen as can the side advertising for the service.

12 November 1985

城巴於1985年初開始使用倫敦寶行走過境路線500號；D36於尖沙咀中間道500號路線之起點準備前往中國深圳，共中國車牌及旁邊的廣告清晰可見。

LEFT: One of the MCW bodied DMSs in the KMB fleet former DMS 1564 now 2D68 now with a new windscreen and flat lower front awaits its departure time at the Star Ferry Kowloon.

12 November 1985

2D68配備原裝MCW車身，然而其擋風玻璃經已被修改，於1985年11月12日駛離尖沙咀天星碼頭。

ABOVE: Bright sunshine is reflected from the windows of the Hong Kong hotel in Middle Road Kowloon on to Argos No. 15 former DMS 1878. The bus carries a promotional livery to encourage visitors to visit Macau and carries blinds for a residents bus service.

12 November 1985

雅高15號 (前倫敦寶1878) 正停於中間道，猛烈的陽光使半島酒店完全反射在車上的玻璃窗上，並披上澳門旅遊的色彩接載失明人士。

CENTRE RIGHT: Former DMS 1878 now Argos No. 15 passes the YMCA as it pulls away from Middle Road Kowloon.

12 November 1985

雅高15號倫敦寶正沿中間道駛經女青年會會址。

RIGHT: A front view of former DMS 2157 now Citybus D36 seen in Middle Road Kowloon and about to depart on the cross border service to Shen Zhen. In the windscreen can be seen many paper permits to allow the bus to access restricted roads in the border area.

12 November 1985

城巴D36爲倫敦寶2157，這天預備行走香港至深圳的路線500號，從D36的擋風玻璃上的許可證之多，可見此車能夠誇越多個禁區。

ABOVE: KMB 2D32 former DMS 1550 leaves the Star Ferry Kowloon in what could be said to be 'standard' KMB condition, the building on the right is Star House in which Citybus had their office for several years.
12 November 1985

2D32帶著標準的九巴色彩駛離天星碼頭，右方的建築物爲星光行，城巴的辦公室亦於1980年代設於這幢大廈。

LEFT: This bus, KMB 2D12, former DMS 1554, would subsequently spend many years in the KMB training fleet. Here it stands outside Star House, Kowloon waiting to depart on route 2c.
12 November 1985

2D12在九巴訓練學校中服務不少光景；在1985年年底，此車仍提供載客服，停於星光行外行走路線2C。

LEFT: Seen from an overhead pedestrian walkway CMB XF 9 former DMS 444 passes along Connaught Road, Central.
12 November 1985

中巴XF9於1985年11月12日駛過干諾道中。

ABOVE: Former DM 1227 was selected by TSW Ltd and Citybus for conversion into a mobile blood donation centre. Although not carried Citybus allocated fleet number D47 for maintenance purposes. Here it awaits custom in Hamilton Street Kowloon adjacent to Kwong Wah hospital. **12 November 1985**
TSW公司於80年代同時購入前倫敦寶1227，後來城巴把此車改成流動捐血站，這天停泊在油麻地廣華醫院側。

BELOW: Front view of DM 1227 showing in particular the offside driver's cab door and the opening for the air conditioning condenser fan behind the front wheel. The towed generator trailer can also be seen. **12 November 1985**
流動捐血站的前幅清楚看到此車的特徵：下層唯一的窗子在駕駛室旁及空，位於此車後端的獨立發電機亦清楚看見。

ABOVE LEFT: Showing the modified front entrance door arrangement on KMB DMSs former DMS 780 now 2D47 stands at the bus terminus under a road flyover at Lai Chi Kok not far from the Head Office of KMB.
13 November 1985
九巴 2D47 的前門的格局經過修改；於 1985 年11月13日停在荔枝角大橋的巴士站。

ABOVE: Another KMB DMS that would see service in the training fleet was former DMS 1551, now KMB 2D18 awaiting the return of the driver at Lai Chi Kok.
13 November 1985
另一部倫敦寶 2D18 (前倫敦寶 1551)，停於荔枝角車站作車長的更替。

LEFT: Also at Lai Chi Kok we find KMB 2D33 former DMS 1541.
13 November 1985
2D33 也在同一天停泊於荔枝角大橋的巴士站內。

BELOW LEFT: KMB 2D100 former DMS 1637 collects passengers in Kwun Tong Road , Kwun Tong. To the left can be seen the flyover and wiring for the MTR.
13 November 1985
2D100 (前倫敦寶 1637) 在觀塘道停頓讓乘客登車，左方爲地下鐵路之高架路段。

BELOW: KMB 2D40 former DMS 1545 seen in Kwun Tong Road.
13 November 1985
九巴 2D40 亦同樣經過觀塘道。

RIGHT: A surprisingly empty stretch of Kwun Tong Road sees KMB 2D81 former DMS 1609 speeding along towards Lok Fu.

13 November 1985

九巴2D81在一段交通異常暢通的觀塘道飛馳，開往樂富。

BELOW: High rise apartments provide the background for KMB 2D46 former DMS 700 seen outside Kowloon Bay MTR station, an older Daimler CVG crosses on the flyover behind.

13 November 1985

2D46於九龍灣地鐵站外駛過，後方的背景為高架的地鐵站。

BELOW: Sandwiched between two generations of front engined vehicle, KMB 2D52 former DMS 1583 is seen outside Kowloon Bay MTR station.

13 November 1985

在兩輛前置引擎車輛之間的九巴2D52，一同駛經九龍灣地鐵站。

RIGHT: Open Top Argos No. 12 former DM 1780 stands on the roof top parking area of the Telford Centre, Kowloon Bay.
13 November 1985
雅高開蓬巴士12號這天前往九龍灣德福花園內頂層停車場。

RIGHT: Standing in front of open top Argos No.12 we find Argos No. 24 which was formerly DMS 301 looking very little different from its time in London.
13 November 1985
位於雅高開蓬巴士12號前方爲雅高24號巴士；其外觀與在倫敦行走的模樣截然不同。

BELOW: Former DMS 685 is now KMB 2D11, it passes another DMS and a duple bodied airport coach as it leaves the Star Ferry terminus, Kowloon.
15 November 1985
2D11爲前倫敦寶685，於1985年11月15日的尖沙咀天星碼頭正越過另一輛倫敦寶及都普車身的機場豪華巴士。

LEFT: An important contract for Citybus is the residents service between City One Shatin and Kowloon Tong railway station, itself an interchange between the MTR and KCRC lines. Here Citybus D26 former DMS 2145 is seen at the station in MTR livery. This bus would later pass to Argos for further service.
15 November 1985
城巴獲得來往沙田第一城至九龍塘鐵路中轉站之路線經營權；這天城巴 D26 披上地鐵的色彩行走該線，後來 D26 轉售至雅高巴士。

LEFT: Also at Kowloon Tong station and operating on the residents service to City One Shatin is Ocean Park liveried DM 1085 now Citybus L19. This bus would be converted to open top in 1988 and renumbered to become No. 5, and in consequence be one of the last two DMSs to see service with Citybus.
15 November 1985
同樣於 1985 年行走沙田第一城至九龍塘鐵路中轉站之城巴倫敦寶爲 L19；在1988年，L19 被改爲開蓬巴士，而編號六改爲 5 號，成爲城巴最後退役的倫敦寶之一。

LEFT: Standing at Kowloon Tong station, Citybus D27 former DMS 2183 was to be one of two vehicles in KCRC shuttle bus livery. It is working the residents service to City One Shatin.
15 November 1985
停於九龍塘之城巴倫敦寶 D27 爲其中一部帶有九鐵色彩的倫敦寶，在同一天接載沙田第一城的居民。

LEFT: At the City One Shatin bus station we find Citybus D32 former DMS 2139. It is evident from the side advertisements and the additional Chinese number plate that this vehicle also works the cross border service to Shen Zhen.

15 November 1985

在沙田第一城車站可見城巴D32，從此車的中國車牌及車旁的宣傳廣告，可見D32亦有行走過境路線。

LEFT: Another vehicle to work on the cross border service 500 to Shen Zhen is Citybus D25 former DMS 2144 seen in the City One Shatin bus station. This bus would be converted to open top in 1988 and renumbered to become No. 6.

15 November 1985.

城巴D25亦有行走跨境路線，在1985年11月15日停於沙田第一城車站；D25後來亦被改爲開蓬巴士，車隊編號則改爲6號。

LEFT: Standing in the corner of the Citybus depot at Tsuen Wan MTR station is DMS 2207 being prepared for service. This bus had been one of two imported by TSW Ltd for intended operation in Macau, but subsequently sold to Citybus. After extensive rebuilding the vehicle would become Citybus 45 and enter service in 1986. It would later pass to Guangzhou, China for further service.

15 November 1985

停在城巴荃灣車廠的倫敦寶爲前倫敦寶2207，此車原來爲TSW公司準備在澳門提供服務，但最後由城巴所購得；經過一番改裝後，在1986年投入服務，成爲城巴45號巴士；後來此車亦再次易手，於1990年代售予廣州第一汽車公司(廣州一汽)。

ABOVE: The Citybus depot at Tsuen Wan MTR station. On the left are the two vehicles originally intended for operation in Macau. Yellow liveried DMS 2207 being prepared for service would become No.45. Next to it is former DMS 2218 now Citybus D44 which would be licensed three days later this month. The grey vehicle at the back is former DMS 2140 which would be the last DMS to enter service with Citybus one year later in November 1986.

15 November 1985

左方兩部倫敦寶爲原來TSW公司準備付運往澳門服役，黃色車身爲城巴45號，另一輛爲D44，後方灰色車身的車輛是前倫敦寶2140，乃最後一輛加入城巴車隊的倫敦寶，於1986年11月正式服務。

CENTRE LEFT: Citybus L14 former DMS 798 in full fleet livery stands in the yard of their depot within the terminus of Tsuen Wan MTR station. The structure behind is the only part of the yard that can be described as under cover.

15 November 1985

城巴L14停泊在荃灣車廠，車廠不少位置爲露天範圍，右方黃色貨櫃爲車廠的辦公室。

LEFT: Nearside view of Citybus L14 former DMS 798 standing in the Tsuen Wan depot yard and showing the removal of the centre exit doors.

15 November 1985

側面的城巴L14，顯示了此車的中門經已被移走。

LEFT: Former DMS 2153 is now D38 in the Citybus fleet. It stands in the Tsuen Wan depot yard showing that its centre exit doors have been retained.

15 November 1985

城巴D38亦停於荃灣車廠，此車的中門則被完好保留。

LEFT: Citybus D33 former DMS 2180 stands in the entrance road to the Tsuen Wan depot. Despite retaining MTR livery it also carries a Chinese number plate to allow operation across the border into Shen Zhen.

15 November 1985

城巴D33停泊在荃灣車廠門前，儘管此車披上地鐵色彩，但同時亦有中國車牌，行走中港過境路線。

BELOW: General view of the Citybus depot at Tsuen Wan, where two former London Transport vehicles meet. Former DMS 798 is now Citybus L14 and on the right is RM 1873 newly arrived from use by CMB and before it was converted and sent on demonstration to Peking.

15 November 1985

城巴車廠的部份景觀；兩部前倫敦巴士停靠在一起，左邊爲L14；右邊爲剛抵港的Routemaster RM1873尚未前往北京試驗行走的模樣。

RIGHT: In 1985 Argos were using a piece of vacant ground adjacent to Tuen Mun road in Tuen Mun to park their vehicles. Here we find Argos No.3 former DMS 663.

15 November 1985

在1985年，雅高巴士亦使用屯門公路旁的空地作爲停泊巴士的地點；同年的11月15日，雅高巴士3號巴士停靠於此。

BELOW RIGHT: In the Tuen Mun parking yard we see former DMS 1642 now Argos No.4 next to Argos No.37 originally Rotherham OET101M in the new yellow livery.

15 November 1985

在屯門的雅高車廠內，可見雅高4號及37號倫敦寶，髹上黃色色彩的37號巴士，以前服務於英國Rotherham公司。

BELOW: Argos No.27 former Tayside 175 stands next to Argos No.25 former DMS 142 in the Tuen Mun parking yard. The DMS retains its centre exit doors and close together headlights.

15 November 1985

雅高27號巴士爲前英國Tayside 175，這天與倫敦寶雅高25號巴士停於屯門車廠；後者的中門及較狹窄距離的車頭燈仍完好無缺。

ABOVE LEFT: Argos No.7 former DMS 1640 stands in their parking area at Tuen Mun.
15 November 1985
雅高7號巴士(前倫敦寶1640)在同一天停靠在屯門車廠內。

ABOVE: Argos No.4 former DMS 1642 also in the Tuen Mun parking area.
15 November 1985
雅高4號巴士(前倫敦寶1642)在同一天亦停在屯門車廠的空地上。

LEFT: Argos No.2 former DMS 606 stands next to Argos No.34 former Rotherham OET104M in the tightly packed Tuen Mun parking area.
15 November 1985
雅高2號巴士(前倫敦寶606)與34號巴士(前Rotherham OET104M)在屯門停泊在一起。

LEFT: The Tuen Mun parking yard used by Argos sees Argos Nos. 25, 27 & 6 former DMS 142, Tayside 175 and DMS 750.
15 November 1985
雅高的25、27及6號前英國巴士一同停置在屯門車廠。

LEFT: Front and rear views of two Argos DMSs at the Tuen Mun parking yard. On the left is Argos No.6 former DMS 750 and on the right is Argos No.2 former DMS 606. In front is Argos No.21 former DMS 184 in Macau Visitors livery.

15 November 1985

倫敦寶的車頭與車尾可見於同一幅照片上；左方爲雅高巴士6號(前倫敦寶750)，右方爲2號巴士(前倫敦寶606)；最前端爲披上澳門旅遊的雅高21號巴士。

LEFT: Ouside the Argos parking yard at Tuen Mun stands Argos No. 3 former DMS 663.

15 November 1985

屯門車廠外的倫敦寶爲雅高3號(前倫敦寶663)。

BELOW: Pausing in Connaught Road Central Citybus D34 former DMS 2171 shows its Ocean park livery. This bus would later pass to Guangzhou for further service.

16 November 1985

於干諾道中稍作停頓的城巴D34披上海洋公園的色彩，此車後來被運往廣州繼續服務。

ABOVE: Open Top Citybus D23 in special livery for the shuttle service between the Star Ferry and the Peak Tram lower terminus. This bus, former DMS 2150 had been purchased by TSW Ltd and was the first permanent open top vehicle to operate in Hong Kong. TSW arranged a five year lease for the vehicle to Citybus. It was also the first DMS in Hong Kong with the two piece 'glider' entrance doors. A photograph of this vehicle being converted in the workshops of Ensignbus appears in the book *DMS ColourScene 1979-1984,* available from the publisher of this book. The bus later saw service in Guangzhou where a new roof was fitted; see photograph later in this book.

17 November 1985

城巴D23披上特別的色彩行走金鐘山頂纜車站至中環天星碼頭的接駁巴士服務；此車原來經TSW公司所購入，城巴向TSW公司租用D23五年，並成爲第一部永久開蓬的巴士在港服務；D23亦爲第一部倫敦寶以兩扇前門的形式在港行走；於1990年代，D23重新蓋上車頂在廣州繼續如常提供服務。

CENTRE LEFT: Leaving the undercover bus station at Admiralty CMB XF 112 former DMS 916 emerges into bright sunshine.

17 November 1985

離開金鐘室內總站的中巴倫敦寶爲XF112。

LEFT: Citybus D43 former DMS 2165 leaves Admiralty bus station showing its all over advertisement livery for Nike. This was another vehicle to pass to Guangzhou for further service and is illustrated later in this book.

17 November 1985

披上Nike色彩的城巴D43離開金鐘車站；在90年代，D43亦被出售往廣州。

LEFT: Citybus operated a shuttle service on behalf of office workers in the JDH Centre located within the old Hung Hom dockyard. Here Citybus D42 former DMS 2178 stands at the other end of the route, Hung Hom Ferry pier.

18 November 1985

城巴提供JDH中心之接駁巴士服務，來往黃埔船塢及紅磡碼頭；D42在1985年11月18日停於紅磡碼頭車站。

LEFT: Another vehicle working the JDH shuttle service is Citybus D41 former DMS 2130 seen here at Hung Hom ferry pier. Another photograph of this vehicle appears later in this book in Guangzhou. In the background can be seen a KMB AEC Regent V.

18 November 1985

另一部停於紅磡碼頭車站行走JDH中心接駁巴士服務的倫敦寶爲D41，遠方的九巴爲AEC Regent V俗稱大水牛巴士。

LEFT: A unique vehicle in the fleet of Argos was their No. 41. This was former DMS 854 the prototype vehicle for the later B20 type fleetlines. This view taken in Wan Hoi Street Kowloon demonstrates the rebuilt rear end that was necessary to reduce external noise.

18 November 1985

攝於紅磡環海街的爲雅高巴士41號；其車尾部份經過一輪重建，目的在於減低噪音。

LEFT: Central bus station from above, CMB XF 148 and 145 former DMs 989 and 998 respectively.

19 November 1985

中巴的XF148(前倫敦寶989)及XF145(前倫敦寶998)在1985年11月19日停於中環車站。

RIGHT: Stanley is a popular resort on the south side of the island. Buses leave frequently from the Central bus station. However this vehicle CMB XF 149 former DM 988 has just arrived from North Point.

19 November 1985

不少巴士來往赤柱與其他地區，在1985年11月19日，中巴XF149剛從北角駛至赤柱。

BELOW RIGHT: Also just arrived at Stanley from North Point is CMB XF 18 former DMS 436.

19 November 1985

XF18在同一天由北角抵達赤柱。

LEFT: The main stopping service from Central to Stanley is route 6, here CMB XF 139 former DM 947 waits for passengers to leave at Stanley village.

19 November 1985

赤柱對外的主要交通爲來往中環至赤柱的6號巴士路線，這天XF139正於赤柱村等候乘客登車。

BELOW LEFT: A very smart CMB XF 122 former DMS 897 arrives at Stanley village on the south side of Hong Kong Island.

19 November 1985

前倫敦寶897的中巴XF122亦駛至南區赤柱村。

ABOVE: Arriving at Ocean Park is Citybus D34 former DMS 2171.

19 November 1985

城巴D34(前倫敦寶2171)駛進海洋公園地區。

LEFT: Outside the main entrance to Ocean Park is Citybus L 18 former DM 1759. The 'L' indicates that the vehicle retains its Leyland engine.

19 November 1985

在海洋公園正門側的倫敦寶爲城巴L18(前倫敦寶1759)，此車亦配置利蘭引擎。

RIGHT: Maintenance Argos style, Argos No.23 former DMS 106 receives attention in their yard at Wan Hoi Street. On the left is the side of No.42 the Seddon Pennine acquired from China Motor Bus.
20 November 1985
前倫敦寶106轉售往雅高巴士後，成爲雅高23號巴士，這天停泊於環海街車廠·旁邊爲從中華巴士購入的薛頓(Seddon)巴士，編號爲42。

BELOW: The Argos depot at Wan Hoi Street had a limited parking area resulting in buses being parked on the pavement, also they were parked close together to prevent theft. Here we see Argos No. 41 the former prototype B20 DMS 854 outside the depot.
20 November 1985
環海街車廠較其他車廠狹窄，故此不少巴士需停泊在旁邊的行人路上，雅高41號巴士(前倫敦寶854)爲其中之一。

BOTTOM: Also outside the Argos depot behind DMS 854 is Argos No. 21 the former DMS 184 in Macau visitors livery.
20 November 1985
在41號巴士旁的倫敦寶爲雅高21號巴士，並披上推廣澳門旅遊的廣告

LEFT: At the back of the line close to a lamppost is Argos No. 22 former DMS 335 in a colourful livery for a residents service operating to Westlands Court.

20 November 1985

停泊在燈柱旁的前倫敦寶335，後來成爲雅高巴士22號

BELOW LEFT: Argos No. 30 the former DMS 2123 parked on the pavement outside the depot in Wan Hoi Street compare this photograph with that taken on 6 November 1984 shown earlier in this book.

20 November 1985

雅高20號巴士在1985年11月停於環海街車廠，我們可對於1984年所攝的雅高20號作出比較

BELOW: Former DM 1819 was re-numbered from No. 16 to No. 18 in 1984, here it stands in the entrance to the Argos depot in Wan Hoi Street in a livery to promote Road Safety. The roof of an open top DMS can be seen stored on the roof of the workshop behind.

20 November 1985

前倫敦寶1819被雅高巴士收購後，編號於1984年由原來的16號改爲18號，這天以道路安全的色彩停於環海街車廠前；從此車的後方看，我們可見一幅開蓬巴士的車頂被安放於工場上

RIGHT: Citybus D40 the former DMS 2134 seen parked in Dyer Avenue, Kowloon in an unusual livery. Compare this with a later photograph in this book taken on 11 November 1990.

20 November 1985

城巴 D40 這天停留於紅磡戴亞街側。

RIGHT: Waiting to depart for Shen Zen China on route 500 we find Citybus D30 former DMS 2146 standing in Middle Road Kowloon. Later in this book this vehicle is seen converted to open top for the Peak Tram shuttle service and it later saw service in Guangzhou.

21 November 1985

前倫敦寶 2146 售予城巴後，這天停泊於中間道，準備服務港深之間的 500 號路線，此車後來被改裝成開蓬巴士，行走山頂纜車接駁線，並於 90 年代售往廣州。

BELOW: A smartly turned out Argos No. 16 former DM 1723 standing in Middle Road Kowloon in full fleet livery, spoilt only by the empty destination blind box.

21 November 1985

雅高巴士 16 號這天停泊在中間道，原來的目的地牌箱空白一片格外有趣。

ABOVE: Argos No. 13 former DM 1727 stands behind the world famous Peninsular Hotel in Middle Road Kowloon.
21 November 1985
雅高巴士13號停泊於享譽全球的半島酒店旁。

CENTRE RIGHT: Daimaru is a large department store in Causeway Bay. Several CMB routes terminate in the streets outside. Here XF 181 former DM 1175 in appropriate livery stands in front of XF 17 former DMS 484.
21 November 1985
銅鑼灣大丸百貨爲中巴銅鑼灣總站的位置，這天 **XF181** 與 **XF17** 一同停靠於此。

RIGHT. CMB XF 17 former DMS 484 stands outside the Daimaru department store in Causeway Bay.
21 November 1985
中巴XF17停泊於大丸百貨前稍作停留

LEFT: CMB XF 99 former DMS 883 stands outside the Daimaru department store in Causeway Bay in an all over advertisement livery for another department store, the Japanese owned SOGO.

21 November 1985

中巴 XF99 在同一天停於大丸百貨巴士站側，然而，XF99 之車身卻披上日資百貨崇光百貨的色彩。

CENTRE LEFT: Numerically the first, CMB XF 1, former DMS 417, was very elusive to photograph. Here it offloads passengers outside the Hong Kong and Shanghai bank in Central.

22 November 1985

XF1 (前 DMS417) 是以編號計算爲首輛中巴倫敦寶在匯豐銀行總行前停定讓乘客下車。

BELOW: Next to the Tram tracks in Queensway is CMB XF 173 former DM 1193.

22 November 1985

XF173 駛經金鐘道的電車路旁。

ABOVE: Pursued by a Metrobus coach in Queensway is CMB XF 190 former DM 1169.
22 November 1985
緊隨著前方都城嘉慕豪華巴士(MC)爲中巴XF190。

CENTRE RIGHT: CMB XF 164 former DM 1192 approaches Central on its way back from Stanley.
22 November 1985
中巴XF164這天由赤柱駛至繁忙的中環。

RIGHT: CMB XF 24 former DMS 482 drops off passengers in Queensway Central. This vehicle had been operating in Hong Kong for over five years and still retains its original windscreen and front upper deck windows.
22 November 1985
這天XF24停於中環金鐘道旁落客，此車在港服務初期，其上下層之前幅玻璃均被保留。

LEFT: CMB XF 176 former DM 1215 after two years service in Hong Kong in Queensway Central.

22 November 1985

中巴XF176於1985年在港服役近兩年，在同年11月下旬駛經金鐘道。

CENTRE LEFT: Also in Queensway Hong Kong is CMB XF 180 former DM 1214.

22 November 1985

XF180在同一天於金鐘道駛過。

BELOW: Alongside the Tram tracks in Queensway is CMB XF 156 former DM 1050 with a new opening windscreen.

22 November 1985

XF156沿金鐘道電車線旁行駛，車窗下層的前幅玻璃經已被更換。

RIGHT: CMB XF 10 former DMS 443 seen in 'Salem' livery in Connaught Road Central.
22 November 1985
XF10 (前倫敦寶443)，帶著全車沙龍香煙色彩抵達干諾道中。

CENTRE RIGHT: One of the first DMSs to enter service in Hong Kong, CMB XF 4 former DMS 407 seen in Murray Road Central on the north coast route 10.
22 November 1985
首批在港服役的倫敦寶 — 中巴XF4這天行走港島北岸線10號，駛至中區美利道。

BELOW: Three DMSs line up in Murray Road Central, leading the group is CMB XF 124 former DM 936, behind is XF 109 former DMS 857 and XF 157 former DM 1071 brings up the rear.
22 November 1985
三輛倫敦寶於美利道成一直線駛過，前方爲XF124；中間爲`前倫敦寶857 (XF109)；後方爲XF157。

ABOVE: Des Voeux Road Central sees CMB XF 60 former DMS 608.
17 November 1986

於 1985年11月22日行經德輔道中爲前倫敦寶608爲中巴的XF60；

CENTRE LEFT: CMB XF 90 former DMS 832 seen in Des Voeux Road Central in 'Salem' livery, behind is XF 96 former DMS 900.
17 November 1986

XF90同樣以全身的沙龍香煙廣告駛經德輔道中，後方爲前倫敦寶900 — XF96。

BELOW: In the same spot, Des Voeux Road Central is CMB XF 191 former DM 1200. This was the last of the penultimate batch received by CMB and was damaged in transit from the UK, accordingly it was returned for repair and re-exported two months later entering Hong Kong service in March 1984.
17 November 1986

XF191駛經中環德輔道中，而XF191爲中巴最後一輛接收之倫敦寶；由於在運輸過程中途損毀，此車需運往英國修理，並重新運抵本港，於1984年3月投入服務。

RIGHT: Beneath one of the many overhead walkways linking office buildings in Central is CMB XF 151 former DM 991 seen in Chater Road.
17 November 1986
XF151在商廈頻密的中環鬧市的遮打道駛過。

BELOW: Rounding the sharp bend outside the Bank of China in Central is CMB XF 1 former DMS 417 still carrying the 'SOGO' livery it had the previous year.
17 November 1986
髹上崇光百貨廣告的XF1在中環中銀大廈掠過。

BOTTOM: Numerically the last CMB DMS is XF 206 former DMS 2096 seen in Des Voeux Road Central. This bus would later be fitted with coach seats and renumbered FC 1, see photograph later in this book.
17 November 1986
中巴最後一輛倫敦寶XF206，這天抵達德輔道中；此車後來被換上全豪華座椅，編號亦更改為FC1。

LEFT: It was unusual for CMB vehicles to carry front advertisements or notices. Here CMB XF 160 former DM 1053 displays this feature as passengers board in Des Voeux Road Central.
17 November 1986
在 1986年11月，XF54 經已爲中巴服務近6年。

CENTRE LEFT: CMB XF 54 former DMS 639 had completed six years service with CMB when seen here in Des Voeux Road Central.
17 November 1986
在 1986年11月，XF54 經已爲中巴服務近6年。

BELOW: Citybus L19 the former DM 1085 stands at the Star Ferry Central awaiting a departure to Ocean Park on the south side of Hong Kong Island. Behind can be seen a former Bournemouth Weymann bodied Fleetline.
17 November 1986
城巴 L19 這天駛至中環天星碼頭，準備駛往海洋公園，後方的巴士爲前利茅夫珍寶。

LEFT: In this view of Argos No.32 former DMS 153 we can see that the lower black stripe has been replaced by a green one. The bus is parked in Dyer Avenue Kowloon. Another photograph of this bus operating in Guangzhou appears later in this book.

17 November 1986

從這個角度看，雅高32號巴士的黑色間條被更改爲綠色，這天停泊在紅磡戴亞街，其後同樣被運往中國廣州繼續行駛。

CENTRE LEFT: Open top DM 1780 is now Argos No. 12. It too carries a green stripe, but the DMS behind retains its black one. It stands outside the depot in Wan Hoi Street.

17 November 1986

雅高12號開蓬巴士的黑色間條同被更改爲綠色，但後方的倫敦寶之間條仍舊爲黑色，同樣停置於環海街車廠。

BELOW: The second open top DMS in the Argos fleet is No. 20 former DM 1743. It stands on the pavement outside the depot in Wan Hoi Street Kowloon.

17 November 1986

雅高巴士第二輛開蓬巴士編號爲20號(前倫敦寶1745)，停泊於環海街車廠旁的行人路。

RIGHT: The Argos depot in Wan Hoi Street, Hung Hom, Kowloon, with three ex London vehicles on show from left to right are No. 33 former MD138, No. 2 former DMS 606 and No. 23 former DMS 106. Note also the roofs from Nos 12 & 20 stored on top of the workshop.

17 November 1986

三輛同爲來自倫敦的雅高二手巴士停於環海街車廠，左方爲33號都城紳佳的Metropolitian，中爲雅高25號(前倫敦寶606)；右方爲23號(前倫敦寶106)，而後方的車頂爲開蓬巴士的改裝工場。

CENTRE RIGHT: Citybus D43 former DMS 2165 working on the shuttle service for the JDH centre seen in 'Nike' livery in Wuhu Street Hung Hom. A photograph of this bus in Guangzhou appears later in this book.

17 November 1986

城巴D43於1986年下旬行走JDH中心的接駁巴士服務並駛經紅磡蕪湖街，此車後來被售往廣州服務廣州市民。

BELOW: Also on the JDH centre shuttle service is Citybus D42 former DMS 2178 seen at Hung Hom Ferry pier.

17 November 1986

同樣行走JDH中心的接駁巴士線爲城巴D42，在同一天駛至紅磡碼頭

LEFT: Very little altered from its time in London is Citybus D43 former DMS 2165 showing its nearside with centre exit doors intact, this bus also saw further operation in Guangzhou. Seen at Hung Hom ferry pier.

17 November 1986

從側面的城巴 D43 看，中門依然被保留，未有被封閉，此車在 1990 年代初被售予廣州一汽，行走廣州市路

RIGHT: Former DM 1746 is now Argos No. 14 seen parked on the pavement in Dyer Avenue Kowloon in full fleet livery, but still with a lower black stripe.

19 November 1986

前倫敦寶 1746 爲雅高巴士 14 號，此車的黑色間條仍得以保留。

LEFT: Prototype B20 type DMS 854 now Argos No. 41 seen parked outside the depot in Wan Hoi Street, Kowloon.

19 November 1986

雅高 41 號巴士 (前倫敦寶 854) 爲 B20 之原型 0，在 1986 年 11 月.19 日停於紅磡環海街。

ABOVE: The two Argos open top vehicles parked next to each other in Wan Hoi Street, Kowloon. No.20 is former DM 1743 and No. 12 is former DM 1780.

19 November 1986

雅高巴士的12號與20號，同樣成爲雅高巴士 第一批開蓬巴士，這天一同停於紅磡環海街車廠內。

CENTRE RIGHT: Argos No. 13 is former DM 1727 and was previously numbered 20. It demonstrates the usual Argos parking arrangement, on the pavement next to a lamppost.

19 November 1986

雅高13號巴士爲原編號爲20號，此車停泊在紅磡海旁的燈塔側。

RIGHT: Citybus D40 former DMS 2134 wearing an all over advertisement for Mild Seven cigarettes seen at Hung Hom ferry pier.

19 November 1986

停於毗連的紅磡碼頭的城巴D40，披上了全幅的萬事發香煙廣告。

LEFT: Demonstrating clearly the modified front door arrangement is CMB XF 166 former DM 1204 leaving the bus station at Stanley Village, note the absence of a front bumper.

19 November 1986

XF166在港行走期間，經已被換上已改善的車門排列，而前方的防撞槓亦被拆除，這天駛離赤柱村。

CENTRE LEFT: CMB XF 64 former DMS 611 has just arrived at Stanley Village.

19 November 1986

中巴XF64這天剛抵達赤柱村。

BELOW: Still with its original close together headlights is CMB XF 35 former DMS 30 at the Stanley Village bus stop.

19 November 1986

仍然裝有舊式車頭燈排列的XF35，在同一天停於赤柱村巴士站內。

157: At the same spot we see CMB XF 86 former DMS 691.
19 November 1986
XF86同時亦駛至赤柱村巴士總站。

CENTRE RIGHT: Later to see service in Guangzhou, but here at Kowloon Tong station we find Citybus D41 former DMS 2130 in 'Mild Seven' cigarettes livery and awaiting to depart on the residents service to City One Sha Tin.
20 November 1986.
不少在港的倫敦寶於90年代被運往廣州繼續行走，城巴D41為其中一部份，於1986年下旬，城巴D41停於九龍塘地鐵站，準備前往沙田第一城。

BELOW: Also at Kowloon Tong on the residents service is Ocean Park liveried Citybus D31 former DMS 2142.
20 November 1986
披上海洋公園色彩的城巴D31同樣駛至九龍塘地鐵站載客。

ABOVE: Still carrying a mainland China number plate is Citybus D28 former DMS 2155, it would later work in Guangzhou, see photograph later in this book. Here it stands at Kowloon Tong station.

20 November 1986

城巴 D28 (前倫敦寶 2155) 同樣抵達九龍塘地鐵站；此車當時附有中國內地車牌，於 90 年代同樣運抵廣州服役。

CENTRE LEFT: Citybus D44 former DMS 2218 would later become Argos 71. Here it stands at Kowloon Tong station in 'Mild Seven' cigarettes livery.

20 November 1986

城巴 D44 (前倫敦寶 2218) 後來成爲雅高巴士 71 號，於 1986 年11月20日，披著萬事發廣告到達九龍塘地鐵站。

LEFT: Citybus D35, the former DMS 2147, would also pass to Argos as their No. 68. Here it stands at Kowloon Tong station awaiting the next departure to City One Sha Tin.

20 November 1986

城巴 D35 (前倫敦寶 2147) 後來亦易手至雅高巴士，同樣在 1986 年11月20 日停泊於九龍塘地鐵站，準備前往沙田第一城。

ABOVE: Citybus D32 former DMS 2139 also with a mainland China number plate arrives at City One Sha Tin.
20 November 1986
同樣具備中國車牌的城巴D32，這天駛至沙田第一城。

CENTRE RIGHT: Standing in the bus station at City One Sha Tin is Citybus D33 former DMS 2180.
20 November 1986
前倫敦寶2180，爲城巴D33，在同一天也停泊於沙田第一城。

RIGHT: Citybus D27 former DMS 2183 stands in City One Sha Tin adjacent to the bus station, behind can be seen some of the many apartment tower blocks that comprise the residential area of City One.
20 November 1986
城巴D27停泊於沙田第一城總站一旁，從後方密集的高樓住宅，可見第一城爲當時香港的一大住宅區。

ABOVE: With a delightful background of hills and apartment buildings we see KMB trainer CM 4727 former DMS 1554 at work having just crossed the river in Sha Tin.

20 November 1986

在1986年11月，九巴倫敦寶訓練巴士CM4727跨越沙田城門河。

LEFT: The late afternoon sunlight creates shadows at the yard used by the KMB training school at Butterfly Valley Road, Lai Chi Kok. On the left is CN 672 former DMS 735 and next to it is CN 315 former DMS 760.

20 November 1986

在九巴蝴蝶谷巴士廠內，不少訓練巴士停泊於此，左方為倫敦寶2D22 (CN672)，右方為2D30 (CN315)。

BELOW: A close up view of KMB Training bus CN 672 former DMS 735 taken with a telephoto lens since access to the yard in Butterfly Valley Road was denied.

20 November 1986

從近距離看九巴訓練巴士2D22 (CN672)。

LEFT: A similar view of KMB Training bus CN 315 former DMS 760 in the Butterfly Valley Road yard.
20 November 1986

169.
從近距離看另一部九巴訓練巴士2D30 (CN315)。

BELOW: About to park up for the night at the Butterfly Valley Road yard is KMB training bus CY 8605 former DMS 605.
20 November 1986

170.
另一部九巴倫敦寶訓練巴士2D104 (CY8605)駛至蝴蝶谷道車廠。

LEFT: Arriving at the yard used by the KMB training school is CN 4313 former DMS 1575. To the left is a prison, hence the security fence.
20 November 1986

九巴倫敦寶訓練巴士2D48 (CN4313)，正駛進蝴蝶谷車廠內，左方爲荔枝角拘留所。

RIGHT: Also arriving at Butterfly Valley Road at the end of the day is KMB training bus CM 4727 former DMS 1554.

20 November 1986

前倫敦寶1554爲九巴倫敦寶訓練車2D12 (CN4727)，在黃昏時間駛至車廠。

RIGHT: The same spot outside the prison sees KMB training bus CN 4588 former DMS 1595 returning to the Butterfly Valley Road for the night.

20 November 1986

在荔枝角拘留所外準備駛入車廠內的訓練巴士2D38 (CN4588)爲前倫敦寶1595。

BELOW: The evening sun casts shadows as KMB Training bus CP 298 former DMS 795 returns home to the KMB training school yard in Butterfly Valley Road.

20 November 1986

不少訓練巴士於黃昏時段回廠，九巴訓練車2D65 (CP298)爲其中之一。

ABOVE: Outside the rear of the Peninsular hotel in Middle Road Kowloon is Citybus D30 former DMS 2146 awaiting a departure to the mainland China city of Shen Zhen.
21 November 1986
停泊於半島酒店後方的中間道的城巴D30於1986年11月21日準備前往深圳。

BELOW: After the departure of DMS 2146 the next bus for Shen Zhen was Citybus D39 former DMS 2149.
21 November 1986
另一部城巴D39亦一同準備就緒服務深圳過境線。

LEFT: Nearside view of Citybus D39 former DMS 2149 showing that the centre exit doors have been retained.

21 November 1986

從另一角度看，可見D39的原來的中門被保留。

ABOVE: Middle Road Kowloon was also used as a convenient pick-up point for charters. Here Argos No. 31 former DMS 2124 is loading up for a day trip.

21 November 1986

九龍中間道爲不少旅遊團體的集合點，同一天，雅高31號準備接載旅遊團團友。

LEFT: The sun reflects off the windows of the Kowloon Hotel behind Argos No. 5 former DMS 1629 as it loads up in Middle Road, Kowloon.

21 November 1986

滿載乘客的雅高5號巴士經過中間道，玻璃窗所反射的建築物爲半島酒店。

RIGHT: Crossing Middle Road Kowloon is Hankow Road and here Argos No. 26 former DMS 406 loads for a private hire day trip. The livery for Beacon Heights shows that the bus is used on a residents service to this new housing development.

21 November 1986

停泊於尖沙咀漢口道的雅高巴士26號準備提供私人租賃服務，其車身的畢架山花園的色彩正表示此車同時爲該住宅區的接駁巴士。

CENTRE RIGHT: Close together headlights distinguish former DMS 106 as an early DMS now Argos No. 23, this was the oldest DMS in the Argos fleet. It is seen in Middle Road Kowloon amongst other Argos vehicles undertaking a private hire.

21 November 1986

早期的倫敦寶的車頭燈距離較窄，而雅高巴士23號具有這特徵，而此車同時爲倫敦寶編號最前的巴士，編號爲 DMS106；這天駛至中間道。

RIGHT: Nearside view of Argos No. 23 former DMS 106 which despite being fifteen years old still looks in fine condition even retaining its push-out opening front upper deck windows.

21 November 1986

於1986年擁有15年車齡的雅高巴士23號，雖上層前幅的擋風玻璃仍被保留，但看來仍歷久常新。

ABOVE: Passengers for Argos Nos. 31 and 26 former DMSs 2124 and 406 spill onto the road in Kowloon at the junction of Middle Road and Hankow Road.
21 November 1986
不少乘客在尖沙咀漢口道與中間道交界從雅高巴士31及26號下車。

RIGHT: Argos No. 5 former DMS 1629 passes Argos No.31 former DMS 2124 in Middle Road Kowloon, compare the front windscreen and upper window treatment between the two vehicles.
21 November 1986
雅高巴士5號正準備越過31號巴士；二者的下層前幅有所不同。

BELOW: The bright sunshine reflects off the glass windows of the Kowloon Hotel on to Argos No. 15 former DMS 1878 in Middle Road Kowloon. Compare this view with that of the same bus taken in a similar spot on 6 November 1984 earlier in this book.
21 November 1986
強烈的陽光使雅高巴士15號的車窗帶上半島酒店的影像。

LEFT: Argos No. 15 former DMS 1878 seen in Salisbury Road Kowloon fully loaded with standing passengers upstairs as it leaves the Peninsular Hotel behind.
21 November 1986
雅高巴士在同一天滿載乘客駛經梳士巴利道。

CENTRE LEFT: CMB XF 16 former DMS 494 had been in service in Hong Kong for over six years when photographed in Paterson Street, Causeway Bay.
21 November 1986
在 1986 年 11 月 21 日，在港行走近 6 年的 XF16，前倫敦寶 494 駛王銅鑼灣百德新街。

LEFT: CMB XF 158 former DM 1066 also stands in Paterson Street, Causeway Bay.
21 November 1986
XF158 在相同的日子駛經繁忙的百德新街。

LEFT: Wearing an all over advertisement livery for the SOGO department store is CMB XF 154 former DM 1057 at the terminus of route 24, Paterson Street, Causeway Bay.

21 November 1986

披上全車崇光百貨廣告的XF154這天行走路線24號，停泊於百德新街巴士總站。

LEFT: Paterson Street is also the terminal point for route 5B. Here CMB XF 179 former DM 1201 waits to take up its next duty.

21 November 1986

XF179這天服務5B路線，同樣停泊在百德新街巴士總站。

RIGHT: Time is fast running out for DMS 698 now KMB 2D13 in Hong Kong, it is seen here in Salisbury Road Kowloon. The following year it would pass to Speedybus and then be one of the first DMSs to operate in Guangzhou.

21 November 1986

在1986年11月，九巴2D13駛經尖沙咀梳士巴利道，翌年，此車亦轉讓予必達巴士，成爲第一批運往廣州服務的倫敦寶。

LEFT: It was relatively rare to find an Argos vehicle parked on the Citybus stand at the Star Ferry, Central, but here we see Argos No. 30 former DMS 2123 doing precisely that.

22 November 1986

相對城巴而言，雅高巴士甚少把巴士停泊在中環天星碼頭；在1986年11月下旬，雅高30號倫敦寶早有地停泊於上址。

BELOW: Outside the Star Ferry Central on the stop normally reserved for CMB route 15 to the Peak is Citybus D37 former DMS 2160. This bus would later pass to Yau Fung Tours for further service as the only DMS in their fleet.

23 November 1986

城巴D37這天停泊於中巴位於天星碼頭之15號巴士站，此車後來轉售予有豐巴士公司，成爲該公司唯一之倫敦寶巴士。

LEFT: CMB XF 34 former DMS 438 was a unique bus. Its front door was converted by Ensign in the UK and the bus was exhibited in the UK by Ensign during 1980, it being the only vehicle from the early batches so modified before export. It is seen here at the North Point terminus of route 10. A photograph of this bus as exhibited by Ensign may be seen in the previous book *'DMS ColourScene 1979 -1984'*, available from the publisher.

23 November 1986

中巴XF34爲一輛較特別的巴士，其前門的重建工程由英國Ensign公司負責，並出席於1980年Ensign車展內；在1986年11月下旬XF34行走中巴10號路線。

LEFT: Bright sunshine at North Point sees CMB XF 73 former DMS 828 with former DMS 915 behind.

23 November 1986

中巴XF73與前倫敦寶915停泊在陽光普照的北角碼頭。

RIGHT: A CMB re-bodied Guy Arab stands behind a very smart CMB XF 117 former DMS 915 at North Point.

23 November 1986

中巴XF117的後方爲中巴已改建的佳牌阿拉伯五型巴士(Guy Arab V)。

BELOW: With a local modification to its front entrance door CMB XF 71 the former DMS 167 shows that its close together front headlights have survived the other modifications at the front. It stands at North Point.

23 November 1986

中巴XF71這天出現於北角碼頭，其車門的格局與及較狹窄的車頭燈距離顯而易見。

RIGHT: CMB XF 118 former DMS 894 had a frontal accident and the upper deck front was rebuilt to become unique in that it had a cream coloured strip between the upper windows. It is seen here as rebuilt at North Point next to XF 33 former DMS 456.
23 November 1986
中巴的XF118經歷交通意外後，其上層的擋風玻璃經過一番改裝，膠邊亦被髹上奶黃色。

BELOW: Side advertisements on CMB XFs were relatively rare. Here CMB XF 119 former DMS 898 displays this feature whilst on lay over at Kennedy Town.
23 November 1986
單幅的橫額廣告在中巴倫敦寶較爲罕有，中巴XF119 (前倫敦寶898) 正髹上此款廣告，停泊於堅尼地城總站。

BELOW: Three former London buses in the Citybus yard at Tsuen Wan. RMs 1288 and 1873 have both recently returned from mainland China. On the right is open top Citybus D23 former DMS 2150 in Peak Tram shuttle bus livery. Just visible at the back is L10 the Volvo Ailsa which had originally been Citybus V1.
24 November 1986
三輛前英國倫敦巴士停泊於荃灣城巴車廠，Routemaster RM1288與RM1873剛從中國試驗行駛完畢回港，右方爲披上山頂纜車廣告的城巴倫敦寶D23；後方爲原來編號V1的富豪艾爾莎L10。

ABOVE: With less than one year before it was to be scrapped KMB 2D40 former DMS 1545 is seen outside Kowloon Bay station.

24 November 1986

攝於1986年11月24日的九巴2D40，出現於九龍灣站外，此車於翌年退役並拆毀。

LEFT: KMB 2D57 former DMS 1594 stops to collect passengers at Kowloon Bay station.

24 November 1986

2D57於九龍灣站外讓乘客登車。

BELOW: Kowloon Bay station also sees KMB 2D53 former DMS 695. By 1986 withdrawals or transfer to the training school had commenced.

24 November 1986

2D53同時出現於九龍灣車站；此車於同年退役並改裝成九巴車長訓練巴士

RIGHT: In the same spot at Kowloon Bay we see KMB 2D55 former DMS 642.

24 November 1986

九巴 2D55 亦於同一天駛過九龍灣站。

RIGHT: Compare the front domes where the different beading distinguishes a body built by MCW or Park Royal. On the left is KMB 2D88 former MCW bodied DMS 1547 on the right is 2D72 which is Park Royal bodied former DMS 800. They stand at the terminus at Tai Hang Tung Estate.

25 November 1986

從倫敦寶車頂的前部分外形，可清楚分辨 Park Royal 或 MCW 車身，左方爲九巴配上 MCW 車身的 2D88；右方爲套用 Park Royal 車身的 2D72，此圖攝於大坑東村巴士總站。

RIGHT: Nearside view of KMB 2D88 former DMS 1547 at Tai Hang Tung Estate showing the rebuilt front entrance door and silver door leaves.

25 November 1986

從側面的九巴 2D88 看，可清晰望見已改建的車門及銀色的門頁。

LEFT: Arriving at Tai Hang Tung Estate is KMB 2D92 former DMS 718.

25 November 1986

正駛進大坑東總站的九巴倫敦寶爲 2D92。

ABOVE: Tai Hang Tung Estate again finds consecutively numbered KMB 2D92 and 2D93 former DMS 718 and 1565 respectively.

25 November 1986

編號順序的九巴倫敦寶 2D92 及 2D93 在 1986 年 11 月 25 日同一時間抵達大坑東總站。

LEFT: Also arriving at Tai Hang Tung Estate is KMB 2D71 former DMS 777.

25 November 1986

2D71 亦隨後駛至大坑東總站。

RIGHT: An AEC Regent V can be seen behind KMB 2D72 former DMS 800 at the Tai Hang Tung Estate terminus.
25 November 1986
停留在大坑東總站的2D72後方的巴士爲九巴AEC大水牛巴士。

CENTRE RIGHT: KMB 2D8 former DMS 725 was numerically the first DMS in the KMB fleet. It is seen here at Tai Hang Tung Estate. The following year it would pass to Speedybus for operation in Guangzhou. See photograph later in this book and compare with that taken on 28 October 1984 earlier in this book.
25 November 1986
以編號釐定，2D8爲九巴身一部倫敦寶，這天同樣駛回大坑東總站，2D8於1987年售予必達巴士於廣州繼續服役。

RIGHT: Rear view of one of the last batch of DMSs received by CMB, XF 193 former DMS 2083 stands at North Point.
25 November 1986
駛至北角碼頭總站的前倫敦寶2083，爲中巴XF193，此乃中巴最後一批引進的二手倫敦寶之一。

LEFT: Arriving at the North Point terminus is CMB XF 146 former DM 978.
25 November 1986
中巴XF144於相近時間駛近北角碼頭巴士總站。

BELOW: The next arrival at North Point is CMB XF 198 former DMS 2097.
25 November 1986
隨後駛進北角碼頭總站的中巴倫敦寶爲XF198。

BOTTOM: A line of DMSs at North Point, headed by CMB XF 193 former DMS 2083 in an all over advertisement livery for City Sports.
25 November 1986
數輛中巴倫敦寶在北角碼頭停泊成一直線，第一輛爲披上全車的運動廣告的XF193。

RIGHT: Ocean Park Hong Kong main entrance sees Citybus L17 former DM 1749 waiting to return to Central.

25 November 1986

城巴L17停泊於海洋公園正門等待接載遊客返回中環。

CENTRE RIGHT: Citybus L19 former DM 1085 outside Ocean Park on the south side of Hong Kong Island.

25 November 1986

城巴L19停泊於港島南區的海洋公園外。

BELOW: Citybus L16 former DM 1745 would later pass to Guangzhou for further service. Here it collects passengers at Ocean Park for the return trip to Central.

25 November 1986

城巴L16停泊於海洋公園外準備接載遊客前往中環；L16於數年後被運往中國廣州行走,掛上內地車牌

RIGHT: CMB XF55 former DMS 618 arrives at North Point ferry bus terminal on route 85. An unusual 'T' shape advert on the offside can just be seen.
25 November 1986
是前倫敦寶618後爲中巴的XF55，在1986年11月25日行走路線85抵達北角碼頭總站.側面較早見的廣告形式清楚可見。

CENTRE RIGHT: Argos No. 31 former DMS 2124 seen in Wan Hoi Street, Hung Hom.
26 November 1986
雅高31號巴士於1986年11月26日停泊在紅磡環海街。

BELOW: The newest DMS in the CMB fleet was XF 205 former DMS 2117 seen here fresh from repaint at Admiralty on express route 721.
27 November 1986
中巴的倫敦寶以編號計算，最後一輛爲XF205，此車於1986年11月經過翻新後行走東區走廊路線721。

LEFT: CMB XF 25 former DMS 424 seen in Chater Road Central.
27 November 1986
XF25在同一天駛過中環遮打道。

CENTRE LEFT: Chater Road Central sees CMB XF 160 former DM 1053 taking on passengers.
27 November 1986
XF160在相若時間駛過中環遮打道，讓乘客登車。

BELOW: Speeding along Chater Road Central is CMB XF 72 former DMS 835 in an all over advertisement livery for Salem cigarettes.
27 November 1986
帶有沙龍香港色彩的XF72在中環遮打道上高速駛過。

LEFT: With a background of tall office buildings CMB XF 52 former DMS 399 pauses in Chater Road Central.

27 November 1986

XF52在高樓林密的遮打道旁稍作停留。

BELOW: Also in Chater Road Central is CMB XF 74 former DMS 825.

27 November 1986

XF74亦同時間出現於中環遮打道。

BOTTOM: CMB XF 98 former DMS 856 indicates that it is about to leave a bus stop at Admiralty adjacent to the shopping area while working express route 721. The original destination blind box can be seen panelled over below the current display.

27 November 1986

中巴XF98 (前倫敦寶856) 於11月27日行走721號快線,這時剛由位於商業區傍金鐘車站駛出;在現用地名指示牌之下是被覆蓋上了的原有地名指示牌。

RIGHT: The KMB training school yard in Butterfly Valley Road, Lai Chi Kok. On the left is CP 3237 former DMS 730 and next to it is CN 315 former DMS 760.
27 November 1986
九巴蝴蝶谷車廠的車長訓練學校的景象：左方爲倫敦寶 CP3237，右方爲 CN315。

BELOW: A beautiful sunny day sees KMB 2D19 former DMS 1577 turning out of Nathan Road towards the Star Ferry terminus.
28 November 1986
九巴 2D19 在陽光燦爛的彌敦道右轉往尖沙咀碼頭的方向。

RIGHT: CMB XF12 former DMS 491 stands at the old Macau Ferry terminal.
28 November 1986
中巴 XF12 在 1986 年 11 月 28 日停泊在舊港澳碼頭前。

LEFT: Citybus D23 former DMS 2150 prepares to depart from the Star Ferry, Central for another short run to the Peak Tram lower terminal. Since the photograph taken on 17 November 1985 the vehicle has received a new flat windscreen and the destination blind box has been panelled over. Another photograph of this bus in Guangzhou appears later in this book.

3 November 1990

城巴 D23 於 1990 年 11 月 30 日準備駛離中環天星碼頭前往山頂纜車站，其擋風玻璃及路線牌箱已被更換，此車其後亦被運往廣州服務。

CENTRE LEFT: Earlier in this book on 21 November 1985 we saw Citybus D30 former DMS 2146 in full fleet livery awaiting to depart to Shen Zhen. Five years later it is seen here at the Star Ferry in open top form on the Peak Tram shuttle service. The conversion work carried out in Hong Kong may be compared with the previous photograph of D23 which was converted in the UK by Ensign.

3 November 1990

在 1990 年，已髹上城巴顏色的 D30 經已轉爲開蓬巴士，行走山頂纜車接駁路線，這天同樣於天星碼頭停留，從以上兩幅圖片，可見由英國 Ensign 公司負責的改建工程與香港巴士公司所改裝之分別。

LOWER LEFT: Another open top conversion carried out by Citybus was to their D20 former DM 1084. Seen here at the Star Ferry awaiting a departure to Ocean Park. Behind may be seen two CMB Guy Arab Vs at the terminus of route 13. The chassis of LX 318 had originally been LW52 delivered to CMB in 1964.

3 November 1990

城巴另一部訓練巴士爲前倫敦寶 1084 (D20)，此車於同一天同樣停留於中環天星碼頭，但準備行走海洋公園路線；後方爲行走中巴 13 號路線的佳牌阿拉伯五型 LX318，此車於 1964 年投入服務。

ABOVE: One of the final batch of fifteen DMSs obtained by CMB was XF 197 former DMS 2060. Seen here in Connaught Road Central in all over advertisement livery for Park and Shop, a local supermarket.
3 November 1990
XF197爲中巴最後一批爲數15部所引入的倫敦寶；於1990年披上百佳超市的廣告駛至干諾道中。

CENTRE RIGHT: Seen in 'ESSO' livery is CMB XF 160 former DM 1053. Passengers scramble aboard at the stop opposite the new Hong Kong and Shanghai Bank in Central.
3 November 1990
中巴XF160 (前倫敦寶1053) 於1990年披上埃索汽油廣告。

RIGHT: Pulling away from the stop in Chater Road is former DM 978 now CMB XF 146.
5 November 1990
剛駛離中環遮打道巴士站爲中巴XF146。

LEFT: An unusual paint scheme adorns CMB XF 180 former DM 1214 in Chater Road, Central.

5 November 1990

XF180 (前 DM1214) 帶著罕見色彩駛過遮打道。

BELOW: Wan Chai ferry terminal with the harbour in the background plays host to CMB XF 167 former DM 1206, alongside is an air conditioned Dennis Condor new a few months earlier.

5 November 1990

XF167 這天停泊於灣仔碼頭，旁邊爲剛投入服務的丹尼士11米禿鷹空調巴士。

LEFT: In 1990 Argos were using a yard on the island of Tsing Yi to house their fleet, their number 30 former DMS 2123 stands near the entrance in the new grey livery, compare this with the photograph on 6 November 1984 of the same vehicle earlier in this book.

6 November 1990

雅高巴士的車廠在1990年遷往青衣島，雅高30號(前 DMS2123)披上灰色車身停泊於車廠門前。請比較稍前同車在1984年11月6日拍攝的照片。

RIGHT: Rudimentary washing facilities in the Argos yard on the island of Tsing Yi. Dominator No.45 ex Tayside BSP479V stands next to No. 72 former Citybus 46 and originally DMS 2140. This had been the last DMS to enter service with Citybus and had been extensively rebuilt. It can be seen in a 1985 photograph earlier in this book in the Citybus yard awaiting restoration.
6 November 1990

青衣車廠內的洗車設施較爲簡陋，雅高45號爲配有East Lancs車身的丹尼士統治者(Dominator)，旁邊爲雅高巴士72號，前身爲城巴46號，原爲DMS2140,是城巴最後引進的二手倫敦寶,並且被廣泛重建。這部巴士在城巴停車場內等待被復原的照片可在本書稍前部分找到。

CENTRE RIGHT: Former DM 1746 now Argos No.14 (CX8531) stands next to former SYPTE DMS lookalike OKW505R (DT1776) in the yard on Tsing Yi.
6 November 1990

雅高14號與49號前SYPTE倫敦寶(DT1776)，一同停於青衣車廠。

BELOW: The Argos parking yard on Tsing Yi sees4 former London Vehicles, from left to right is former MD66, DMS 153 with headlights close together, DMS 1878 and DMS 798 which had been obtained from Citybus earlier in the year (see earlier photographs in this book).
6 November 1990

在雅高青衣廠內，分別有四部前倫敦的巴士：左至右爲MD66 (雅高36號)，前倫敦寶153, 1878及798。

LEFT: Argos No.6 former DMS 750 in the Tsing Yi yard next to former South Yorkshire PTE OKW521R, both vehicles retain their original windscreens.

6 November 1990

雅高巴士6號停於青衣廠內，隔壁爲SYPTE521R (雅高48號)，兩者的擋風玻璃仍被保留。

CENTRE LEFT: Argos No. 69 formerly Citybus D14 and originally DMS 798 seen at Tsing Yi.

6 November 1990

城巴D14售予雅高後，編號爲69，同樣於青衣島出現。

BELOW: A general view of the Argos parking yard on the island of Tsing Yi.

6 November 1990

雅高巴士的青衣廠址的格局。

ABOVE: Argos No.26 former DMS 406 stands next to former Tayside 175 in the Tsing Yi parking yard.

6 November 1990

雅高巴士26號與雅高巴士27號(Tayside175)一同停於青衣廠。

LEFT: Argos No.1 former DMS 626 stands in the Tsing Yi parking yard. Stickers in the windscreen indicate that this vehicle is employed on contact work for the Hong Kong United Dockyard.

6 November 1990

雅高巴士1號爲倫敦寶626，擋風玻璃前的招紙說明此車爲香港聯合船塢所租用。

BELOW: Leaving the stop in Chater Road is CMB XF 187 former DM 1164.

7 November 1990

離開遮打道車站的倫敦寶爲中巴XF187。

LEFT: One of the last batch of DMS vehicles supplied to CMB is XF 193 former DMS 2083, the rebuilt single width front door can be clearly seen and the bus advertises Craven A cigarettes as it drives through Central.
7 November 1990
XF193之前門已改為單摺式的形態，此車披上香煙廣告駛至干諾道中。

CENTRE LEFT: CMB XF 164 former DM 1192 seen in Connaught Road Central on busy route 6 to Stanley in an all over advertisement livery for Kent cigarettes. **7 November 1990**
XF164披上健牌香煙廣告行走繁忙的干諾道中，行駛來往中環至赤柱之6號路線。

BELOW: A line up of CMB training buses parked at North Point Ferry for their lunch break. Leading the queue is T 19 former DMS 557. The additional mirror for the use of the instructor behind the drivers cab window can be seen.
7 November 1990
數輛倫敦寶於午餐時段停泊成一直線，前排為中巴訓練巴士T19，後方所附加的倒後鏡清晰可見，為導師所專用。

RIGHT: Also at North Point Ferry is CMB XF 122 former DMS 897 on busy route 10 which runs along the north coast of Hong Kong Island.

7 November 1990

中巴 XF122 於北角碼頭準備行走北岸路線 10 號。

CENTRE RIGHT: Parked on the ramp between different levels of the Chai Wan multi storey bus garage is CMB XF 190 former DM 1169.

8 November 1990

停泊於中巴柴灣車廠內一段斜坡的倫敦寶爲 XF190。

BELOW: One of several yards at Chai Wan sees withdrawn CMB XF 2 former DMS 472 with various mechanical parts removed.

8 November 1990

在中巴柴灣另一車廠，可見已退役的 XF2，車上部分零件被移走。

ABOVE: Purple liveried CMB XF 179 former DM 1201 parked in a yard at Chai Wan. Alongside is LF 58, by coincidence both vehicles were new in November 1975.

8 November 1990

披上紫色色彩的XF179停於柴灣車廠，旁邊爲中巴XF58，無獨有偶，XF179與LF58同樣於1975年11月披入服務。

CENTRE LEFT: In mid 1988 former CMB XF 206 numerically the last DMS in the CMB fleet was converted into a 'coach' by the fitting of high backed seats for use on express services from Central to the south side of the island. It was re-numbered to become FC1 (Fleetline coach) and received 'coach' livery. It was originally DMS 2096 and is seen here at the southern terminus of route 262, Chung Hom Kok.

8 November 1990

1988年中，中巴XF206正式改裝成豪華巴士，換上高背座椅及豪華巴士色彩，編號爲FC1；主要行走中環至南區之特快路線，這天駛至舂坎角巴士總站，正行走262路線。

LEFT: Two former DMSs in Central. CMB XF 152 former DM 1058 is passed by XF 128 former DMS 911.

9 November 1990

在1990年11月9日在中環拍攝此照時, XF128正越過鄰邊的XF152。

RIGHT: Showing clearly the front entrance door conversion is CMB XF 112 former DMS 916 at the terminus of route 83, Chai Wan bus station.

9 November 1990

停在柴灣總站的XF112，於1990年11月9日行走路線83，其前門已改裝後的模樣清晰可見。

BELOW RIGHT: UNY liveried CMB XF 49 former DMS 659 stand in Chai Wan bus station.

9 November 1990

XF49髹上UNY百貨公司廣告停於柴灣巴士總站。

ABOVE: The residential area on the south side of the island at Repulse Bay provides the background for CMB XF 42 former DMS 413 in an attractive livery for Kent cigarettes.

10 November 1990

XF42披上健牌香煙廣告駛往南區淺水灣住宅區。

RIGHT: The side of the bus proclaims that Shopping is a Pleasure at the Park and Shop supermarkets. CMB XF 53 former DMS 617 is collecting passengers at Repulse Bay for the return journey to Central.

10 November 1990

帶有百佳超市色彩的XF53這天於淺水灣車站讓乘客登車。

ABOVE: CMB XF 202 former DMS 2075 about to pass another DMS at Repulse Bay on the south side of Hong Kong Island.

10 November 1990

XF202於淺水灣準備越過另一部倫敦寶。

LEFT: The second oldest DMS in the CMB fleet is XF 35 the former DMS 30 seen here outside Pacific Place a shopping and office complex adjacent to Admiralty. Compare this photograph with that taken on 31 October 1984 and it is apparent that the headlights have been re-positioned.

10 November 1990

前倫敦寶30爲中巴XF35，於1990年11月9日行經金鐘太古廣場，當時的XF35的車頭燈距離經已被修改。

BELOW: Citybus D30 former DMS 2146 seen from above carries a full load of visitors en route to the Peak Tram lower terminal.

11 November 1990

城巴D30載滿乘客前往山下纜車站。

RIGHT: Leaving Admiralty bus station for Ocean Park is Citybus D40 former DMS 2134.

11 November 1990

城巴 D40 駛離金鐘站前往旅遊名勝海洋公園。

LEFT: Citybus D45 former DMS 2207 was one of two vehicles purchased by TSW Ltd for operation in Macau, but sold to citybus when that deal failed to be concluded. It stands at Kowloon Tong station in Ocean Park livery. This bus would later be converted to open top and than gain a new roof when sent for further operation in Guangzhou, see photograph later in this book.

11 November 1990

城巴 D45 前身爲澳門 TSW 公司所引入之倫敦寶之一，後來易手至城巴；1990 年披上海洋公園的色彩出現於九龍塘地鐵站，其後並改裝成開蓬巴士；於 1990 年代，此車重新蓋上車頂運上廣州繼續服務。

BELOW: Various vehicles in the Citybus No.1 yard at Fo Tan from left to right are former DMSs 2134, 1759, 1085 and 789.

12 November 1990

數部城巴倫敦寶停泊於火炭車廠；由左至右分別爲倫敦寶 2134，1759，1085 及 789。

ABOVE: Both these vehicles would pass to Guangzhou for further service, former DMS 2207 stands in front of former DMS 2171 in the Citybus yard at Fo Tan.

12 November 1990

在火炭廠內的倫敦寶2207及2171，在1990年代轉手至廣州一汽服務國內市民。

CENTRE LEFT: Working on the JDH contract is Citybus 42, former DMS 2178, at Hung Hom ferry pier, it would later move north to Guangzhou.

13 November 1990

城巴D42同樣爲JDH公司服務，同樣稍停於紅磡碼頭。

LEFT: Another vehicle on the JDH contract on this day was Citybus D15 former DMS 796 seen at Hung Hom ferry pier before it too passed to Guangzhou.

13 November 1990

D15在同一天亦行走JDH公司的員工巴士路線，此車與不少城巴倫敦寶的出路相同，同樣售至廣州的巴士公司服務。

LEFT: At the other end of the route, the JDH Centre we see Citybus 43 former DMS 2165 standing in front of Citybus D42 former DMS 2178.
13 November 1990
爲 JDH 公司服務的城巴 45，這天停於黃埔船廠車站，前方爲倫敦寶 D42。

CENTRE LEFT: Open top former DM 1085 now Citybus D19 passes into the shade along Harcourt Road, Central in Panda livery.
13 November 1990
城巴 D19 改成開蓬巴士後，於 1990 年 11 月 13 日駛經中環夏慤道，並披上熊貓色彩示人。

BELOW: By 1990 the KMB Training School had re-located to the roof of the multi storey garage in Sha Tin. Here CV9753 former 2D101 and originally DMS 794 is seen on a training run outside the garage.
13 November 1990
於 1990 年，九巴訓練學校校址遷往沙田車廠內，前2D101 (CV9753)，於沙田車廠外駛過。

RIGHT: On the roof of Sha Tin garage we find KMB training vehicles CN4375 and CM8752 former 2D45 and 2D21 originally DMSs 1598 and 765 respectively.

13 November 1990

九巴訓練車倫敦寶 CN4375 (2D45) 及 CM8752 (2D21) 停於沙田車廠內

BELOW: Students alight from KMB training bus CM8999 former 2D18 and originally DMS 1551 and return to the office within Sha Tin garage.

13 November 1990

CM8999 (2D18) 駛入沙田車廠內

RIGHT: As dusk approaches KMB training vehicles return to their home on the roof of Sha Tin garage. CP3237 formerly 2D75 and originally DMS 730 waits to park up for the night.

13 November 1990

CP3237 (2D75) 準備駛入九巴訓練學校內

LEFT: A student carries out some last minute manoeuvring in preparation for his test the following day using KMB training bus CV9753 former 2D101 and originally DMS 794, note that the rear part of the front door remains intact unlike that pictured on CM8999.

13 November 1990

九巴學員正駕駛著倫敦寶訓練巴士，此車的前門後部分仍保持原貌

CENTRE LEFT: Argos No.70 formerly Citybus D36 and originally DMS 2157 swings around the roundabout near Kwun Tong ferry.

15 November 1990

前城巴D36爲後來雅高巴士70號，這天駛經觀塘碼頭外的迴旋處。

BELOW: Argos No. 51 former SYPTE DMS OKW513R seen in their Tsing Yi yard.

15 November 1990

雅高51號爲前South Yorkshire PTE倫敦寶，這天停泊於青衣車廠。

ABOVE: The highest numbered DMS in the Argos fleet is No.74 seen here in their Tsing Yi yard still carrying fleet number 38 of its previous owner Citybus. This bus was originally DMS 2153 and was acquired from Citybus in September 1990.

15 November 1990

雅高74號應為該車隊的最後一部倫敦寶，但它仍然保留原來的城巴編號38。此車於1990年9月由城巴購入，這天同樣停在青衣廠一旁。

RIGHT: Argos No.2 former DMS 606 stands in their Tsing Yi yard.

15 November 1990

雅高巴士2號為前倫敦寶606，這天亦停於雅高位於青衣車廠。

BELOW: The Tsing Yi yard of Argos with No. 41 the prototype B20 DMS 854, open top No. 20 former DMS 1743 and No. 7 former DMS 1640.

15 November 1990

不少雅高巴士的倫敦寶分別停於青衣車廠，由左至右為41號，20號開蓬巴士及7號。

廣州 Guangzhou

RIGHT: Following a great deal of information from my friend Lennox MacEwan, a day trip was made to Guangzhou in 1992 to see the former DMSs. The first to greet me was former Citybus D23 originally DMS 2150 with a new square roof operating as fleet No. 12-1374 with Guangzhou Number One Bus Company. The number of people in the bus station made taking photographs very difficult.

5 May 1992

前城巴 D23 於 1992 年 5 月服務廣州一汽時，蓋上全新方形的車頂，編號爲 12-1374，由於候車的乘客眾多，故此拍攝此照時倍感困難。

LEFT: Another view of 12-1374 former DMS 2150 as it tried to avoid people while leaving the bus station in Guangzhou, it was either a long route or it suffered mechanical problems because it never returned that day.

5 May 1992

從另一角度看服務廣州的前城巴的 D23。

BELOW: This is thought to be DMS 725 numerically the first in the KMB fleet 2D8. Standing in Guangzhou bus station carrying fleet No. 1306 this was one of the first double deck vehicles to operate in Guangzhou on hire from Speedybus. Note the new offside door behind the staircase.

5 May 1992

此車可能爲前九巴 2D8，爲第一批服務廣州的倫敦寶之一，車門被改爲右方於樓梯之後端。

LEFT: Rear view of Guangzhou Number One Bus Company 1306 thought to be DMS 725 in the bus station.

5 May 1992

廣州一汽的1306的背面的外貌；此車正停泊於廣州之車站內。

ABOVE: Earlier in this book are several pictures of DMS 2207 whilst operating for Citybus. Here it is again in Guangzhou operating with Guangzhou Number One Bus Company as their number 12-1382. It too has new square roof having been converted to open top whilst in Hong Kong.

5 May 1992

城巴45號於1992年在廣州一汽服務，編號爲12-1382；在港服務期間城巴45爲開蓬巴士，但至廣州服務時，車頂被重建過來。

ABOVE RIGHT: Guangzhou Number One Bus Company 12-1382 former Citybus 45 and originally DMS 2207 stands in Guangzhou bus station.

5 May 1992

廣州一汽12-1382於1992年5月5日停於車站內。

RIGHT: Seen In Guangzhou traffic is Guangzhou Number One Bus Company No. 5-1358, previously Citybus 41 and originally DMS 2130.

5 May 1992

城巴前41號在廣州一汽的編號爲5-1358，這天服務於廣州市之道路中

LEFT: Still retaining its close together headlights is DMS 153 now operating with Guangzhou Number One Bus Company as their 12-1389 seen in Guangzhou traffic. This was one of four vehicles obtained by Citybus from Argos in order to make up the correct number of vehicles required as part of the deal arranged by Citybus with Guangzhou Number One Bus Company.

5 May 1992

前倫敦寶(雅高32)於廣州一汽行走的時期，其舊式的車頭燈形態未有作出改動；部份雅高巴士倫敦寶(包括此車在內)在易手的過程，經由城巴作代理人，從而解決部份有關編號的問題。

CENTRE LEFT: Rear of DMS 153 seen in Guangzhou while operating with Guangzhou Number One Bus Company as their 12-1389.

5 May 1992

前倫敦寶153在廣州一汽的號碼爲12-1389。

BELOW LEFT: Cyclists predominate in this Guangzhou street scene. Former DMS 789 now Guangzhou Number One Bus Company No. 5-1357 approaches the bus station, this bus was previously L22 in the Citybus fleet.

5 May 1992

前城巴L22在單車滿街的路上準備駛至車站，其編號爲5-1357。

BELOW: Guangzhou Number One Bus Company 5-1358 former DMS 2130 stands in the bus station ahead of former Derby Dominator GTO104V. Compare this with the photograph of the same bus taken on 18 November 1985 seen earlier in this book.

5 May 1992

前城巴D41於廣州一汽之編號爲5-1358，後方爲丹尼士統治者(Dominator)

ABOVE: Leaving Guangzhou bus station is DMS 2165 formerly with Citybus as D43 and now Guangzhou Number One Bus Company 5-1359.

5 May 1992

前城巴 D43 正駛離廣州巴士站，其號碼爲 5-1359。

TOP RIGHT: Former DMS 2155 is now 12-1376 with Guangzhou Number One Bus Company and it too has a new square roof when seen in Guangzhou bus station.

5 May 1992

前倫敦寶 2155 在廣州一汽的號碼爲 12-1376，車頂再次被裝上。

ABOVE RIGHT: Guangzhou Number One Bus Company 5-1357 is former Citybus L22 and originally DMS 789. It advertises Craven A cigarettes while standing in the bus station.

5 May 1992

廣州一汽之 5-1357 爲前城巴 L22，披上大幅的香煙廣告。

RIGHT: Guangzhou Number One Bus Company 12-1381 seen outside the bus station is another of the four vehicles obtained from Argos in whose fleet it was No.14, it still carries its Hong Kong registration plate on the front. This bus was originally DM 1746.

5 May 1992

廣州一汽12-1381爲前雅高巴士14，此車同樣以城巴作代理人轉售予一汽，其香港之車牌仍被保留。請比較在 1990 年 11 月13 日拍攝的同車照片。

INDEX – Buses are indexed by London Transport fleet number, followed by the date on which that bus was photographed, each caption showing the date for easy reference with all photos arranged in date order.

For ease of reference, where more than one date is given, the second and subsequent dates are offset to the right to highlight this.